Ferlinghetti's Greatest Poems

Lawrence Ferlinghetti

Ferlinghetti's Greatest Poems

EDITED BY NANCY J. PETERS

A NEW DIRECTIONS BOOK

The painting of the author by Hollis Holbrook
was photographed by John Perino.

Manufactured in the United States of America
New Directions Books are printed on acid-free paper
First published as a New Directions Book in 2017

Library of Congress Cataloging in Publication Data
Names: Ferlinghetti, Lawrence, author. | Peters, Nancy J. (Nancy Joyce), editor.
Title: Ferlinghetti's greatest poems / Lawrence Ferlinghetti ; edited by Nancy J. Peters.
Description: New York : New Directions Publishing, 2017.
Identifiers: LCCN 2017014742 | ISBN 9780811227124 (hardcover : acid-free paper)
Classification: LCC PS3511.E557 A6 2017 | DDC 811/.54—dc23
LC record available at https://lccn.loc.gov/2017014742

2 4 6 8 10 9 7 5 3 1

New Directions Books are published for James Laughlin
by New Directions Publishing Corporation
80 Eighth Avenue, New York 10011

For Julie, Lorenzo, and Kate

Contents

A FAR ROCKAWAY OF THE HEART (1998)

HOW TO PAINT SUNLIGHT (2001)

BLASTS CRIES LAUGHTER (2014)

NEW AND UNCOLLECTED

In Paris in a loud dark winter
                    when the sun was something in Provence
when I came upon the poetry
                    of René Char
        I saw Vaucluse again
                        in a summer of sauterelles
    its fountains full of petals
                        and its river thrown down
        through all the burnt places
                        of that almond world
    and the fields full of silence
                        though the crickets sang
            with their legs
                    And in the poet's plangent dream I saw
no Lorelei upon the Rhone
                    nor angels debarked at Marseilles
but couples going nude into the sad water
                    in the profound lasciviousness of spring
    in an algebra of lyricism
                    which I am still deciphering

* * *

And the Arabs asked terrible questions
and the Pope didn't know what to say and the people
ran around in wooden shoes asking which was the
head of Midas facing and everyone said

No instead of Yes

While still forever in the Luxembourg
gardens in the fountains of the Medici were the
fat red goldfish and the fat white goldfish
and the children running around the pool
pointing and piping
Des poissons rouges!
Des poissons rouges!

but they ran off
and a leaf unhooked itself
and fell upon the pool
and lay like an eye winking
circles

and then the pool was very
still
and there was a dog
just standing there
at the edge of the pool
looking down
at the tranced fish

and not barking
                    or waving its funny tail or
                                        anything
                    so that
                         for a moment then
               in the late November dusk
silence hung like a lost idea
                         and a statue turned
                                        its head

                    * * *

                    Sorolla's women in their picture hats
stretched upon his canvas beaches
                            beguiled the Spanish
                    Impressionists

        And were they fraudulent pictures
                                of the world
            the way the light played on them
                                    creating illusions

    of love?

            I cannot help but think
                            that their 'reality'
was almost as real as
                my memory of today

            when the last sun hung on the hills
            and I heard the day falling
                like the gulls that fell
                almost to land

        while the last picnickers lay
                    and loved in the blowing yellow broom
resisted and resisting
                tearing themselves apart

                            again … again

                        until the last hot hung climax
which could at last no longer be resisted
                                        made them moan

        And night's trees stood up

                        * * *

Fortune
has its cookies to give out
which is a good thing
since it's been a long time since
that summer in Brooklyn
when they closed off the street
one hot day
and the
FIREMEN
turned on their hoses
and all the kids ran out in it
in the middle of the street
and there were
maybe a couple dozen of us
out there
with the water squirting up
to the
sky
and all over
us
there was maybe only six of us
kids altogether
running around in our
barefeet and birthday
suits
and I remember Molly but then

the firemen stopped squirting their hoses
all of a sudden and went
back in
their firehouse
and
started playing pinochle again
just as if nothing
had ever

happened
while I remember Molly
looked at me and

ran in
because I guess really we were the only ones there

* * *

It was a face which darkness could kill
                              in an instant
   a face as easily hurt
                by laughter or light

   'We think differently at night'
                    she told me once
lying back languidly

                    And she would quote Cocteau

'I feel there is an angel in me' she'd say
                    'whom I am constantly shocking'

   Then she would smile and look away
            light a cigarette for me
                         sigh and rise
and stretch
         her sweet anatomy

                    let fall a stocking

                    * * *

HEAVEN ...

Heaven

was only half as far that night

at the poetry recital

listening to the burnt phrases

when I heard the poet have

a rhyming erection

then look away with a

lost look

'Every animal' he said at last

'After intercourse is sad'

But the back-row lovers

looked oblivious

and glad

* * *

The world is a beautiful place
                    to be born into
if you don't mind happiness
                not always being
                        so very much fun
    if you don't mind a touch of hell
                now and then
        just when everything is fine
                        because even in heaven
                they don't sing
                all the time

    The world is a beautiful place
                    to be born into
    if you don't mind some people dying
                        all the time
            or maybe only starving
                        some of the time
        which isn't half so bad
                    if it isn't you

Oh the world is a beautiful place
                    to be born into
        if you don't much mind
                    a few dead minds
        in the higher places
                    or a bomb or two
        now and then

                    in your upturned faces
          or such other improprieties
                              as our Name Brand society
                    is prey to
                         with its men of distinction
          and its men of extinction
                              and its priests
               and other patrolmen
                                   and its various segregations
          and congressional investigations
                              and other constipations
               that our fool flesh
                    is heir to

     Yes the world is the best place of all
                              for a lot of such things as
          making the fun scene
                         and making the love scene
and making the sad scene
                    and singing low songs and having
                                        inspirations
     and walking around
                    looking at everything
                              and smelling flowers
     and goosing statues
                    and even thinking
                              and kissing people and
          making babies and wearing pants

                              and waving hats and
                    dancing
                              and going swimming in rivers
                on picnics
                    in the middle of the summer
          and just generally
                    'living it up'

Yes
     but then right in the middle of it
                         comes the smiling
                                        mortician

                         * * *

Reading Yeats I do not think
                            of Ireland
but of midsummer New York
                            and of myself back then
        reading that copy I found
                       on the Thirdavenue El

      the El
           with its flyhung fans
    and its signs reading
                SPITTING IS FORBIDDEN

      the El
           careening thru its thirdstory world
    with its thirdstory people
                in their thirdstory doors
  looking as if they had never heard
                      of the ground

    an old dame
               watering her plant
  or a joker in a straw
            putting a stickpin in his peppermint tie
and looking just like he had nowhere to go
                      but coneyisland

    or an undershirted guy
              rocking in his rocker

watching the El pass by
            as if he expected it to be different
   each time

      Reading Yeats I do not think
                of Arcady
and of its woods which Yeats thought dead
                   I think instead
     of all the gone faces
           getting off at midtown places
   with their hats and their jobs
   and of that lost book I had
          with its blue cover and its white inside
where a pencilhand had written
         HORSEMAN, PASS BY!

In Goya's greatest scenes we seem to see
                              the people of the world
          exactly at the moment when
               they first attained the title of
                              'suffering humanity'
          They writhe upon the page
                         in a veritable rage
                                   of adversity
               Heaped up
                    groaning with babies and bayonets
                                   under cement skies
               in an abstract landscape of blasted trees
                    bent statues bats wings and beaks
                         slippery gibbets
                    cadavers and carnivorous cocks
               and all the final hollering monsters
                    of the
                              'imagination of disaster'
               they are so bloody real
                              it is as if they really still existed

     And they do
               Only the landscape is changed
     They still are ranged along the roads
          plagued by legionnaires
                         false windmills and demented roosters

We are the same people
                    only further from home
          on freeways fifty lanes wide
                    on a concrete continent
                              spaced with bland billboards
          illustrating imbecile illusions of happiness

                    The scene shows fewer tumbrils
                              but more strung-out citizens
                                        in painted cars
                    and they have strange license plates
                    and engines
                              that devour America

                              * * *

Sometime during eternity
                              some guys show up
and one of them
              who shows up real late
                              is a kind of carpenter
          from some square-type place
                              like Galilee
          and he starts wailing
                              and claiming he is hip
          to who made heaven
                              and earth
                                    and that the cat
              who really laid it on us
                              is his Dad

          And moreover
              he adds
                  It's all writ down
                              on some scroll-type parchments
              which some henchmen
                              leave lying around the Dead Sea somewheres
                  a long time ago
                              and which you won't even find
for a coupla thousand years or so
                              or at least for
          nineteen hundred and fortyseven
                              of them
                  to be exact

                        and even then
nobody really believes them
                        or me
                              for that matter

You're hot
              they tell him
And they cool him
They stretch him on the Tree to cool

              And everybody after that
                              is always making models
              of this Tree
                        with Him hung up
and always crooning His name
                              and calling Him to come down
              and sit in
                        on their combo
        as if he is the king cat
                        who's got to blow
        or they can't quite make it
     Only he don't come down
                              from His Tree
  Him just hang there
                on His Tree
                        looking real Petered out
                and real cool
                        and also

28

according to a roundup

　　　　　　　　of late world news

from the usual unreliable sources

　　　　　　　　　　real dead

* * *

What could she say to the fantastic foolybear
and what could she say to brother
and what could she say
                    to the cat with future feet
and what could she say to mother
after that time that she lay lush
                        among the lolly flowers
    on that hot riverbank
            where ferns fell away in the broken air
                of the breath of her lover
    and birds went mad
                    and threw themselves from trees
to taste still hot upon the ground
                        the spilled sperm seed

* * *

See
    it was like this when
                we waltz into this place
a couple of far out cats
                is doing an Aztec two-step
And I says
            Dad let's cut
but then this dame
                comes up behind me see
                        and says
                You and me could really exist
Wow I says
            Only the next day
            she has bad teeth
                and really hates
                        poetry

                    * * *

Don't let that horse
                eat that violin
    cried Chagall's mother
                        But he
            kept right on
                        painting
And became famous
And kept on painting
                The Horse With Violin In Mouth
And when he finally finished it
he jumped up upon the horse
                        and rode away
        waving the violin
And then with a low bow gave it
        to the first naked nude he ran across

And there were no strings
                attached

                    * * *

Constantly risking absurdity
                              and death
            whenever he performs
                        above the heads
                                    of his audience
      the poet like an acrobat
                        climbs on rime
                                    to a high wire of his own making
and balancing on eyebeams
                        above a sea of faces
            paces his way
                        to the other side of day
      performing entrechats
                        and sleight-of-foot tricks
and other high theatrics
                        and all without mistaking
            any thing
                        for what it may not be

      For he's the super realist
                        who must perforce perceive
            taut truth
                        before the taking of each stance or step
      in his supposed advance
                        toward that still higher perch
where Beauty stands and waits
                        with gravity
                                    to start her death-defying leap

And he
      a little charleychaplin man
               who may or may not catch
       her fair eternal form
             spreadeagled in the empty air
      of existence

* * *

In woods where many rivers run
                        among the unbent hills
    and fields of our childhood
                    where ricks and rainbows mix in memory
although our 'fields' were streets
                    I see again those myriad mornings rise
    when every living thing
                        cast its shadow in eternity
    and all day long the light
                    like early morning
        with its sharp shadows shadowing
                            a paradise
                that I had hardly dreamed of
                        nor hardly knew to think
        of this unshaved today
                    with its derisive rooks
        that rise above dry trees
                    and caw and cry
    and question every other
            spring and thing

                    * * *

35

The pennycandystore beyond the El
is where I first
        fell in love
                with unreality
Jellybeans glowed in the semi-gloom
of that September afternoon
A cat upon the counter moved among
                the licorice sticks
      and tootsie rolls
   and Oh Boy Gum

Outside the leaves were falling as they died

A wind had blown away the sun

A girl ran in
Her hair was rainy
Her breasts were breathless in the little room

Outside the leaves were falling
         and they cried
                Too soon! too soon!

* * *

That 'sensual phosphorescence

                                    my youth delighted in'

  now lies almost behind me

                            like a land of dreams

           wherein an angel

                  of hot sleep

        dances like a diva

                    in strange veils

        thru which desire

                  looks and cries

And still she dances

              dances still

  and still she comes

                at me

                  with breathing breasts

     and secret lips

          and (ah)

                bright eyes

* * *

Dove sta amore
Where lies love
Dove sta amore
Here lies love
The ring dove love
In lyrical delight
Hear love's hillsong
Love's true willsong
Love's low plainsong
Too sweet painsong
In passages of night
Dove sta amore
Here lies love
The ring dove love
Dove sta amore
Here lies love

* * *

Christ climbed down
from His bare Tree
this year
and ran away to where
there were no rootless Christmas trees
hung with candycanes and breakable stars

Christ climbed down
from His bare Tree
this year
and ran away to where
there were no gilded Christmas trees
and no tinsel Christmas trees
and no tinfoil Christmas trees
and no pink plastic Christmas trees
and no gold Christmas trees
and no black Christmas trees
and no powderblue Christmas trees
hung with electric candles
and encircled by tin electric trains
and clever cornball relatives

Christ climbed down
from His bare Tree
this year
and ran away to where
no intrepid Bible salesmen
covered the territory

in two-tone cadillacs
and where no Sears Roebuck creches
complete with plastic babe in manger
arrived by parcel post
the babe by special delivery
and where no televised Wise Men
praised the Lord Calvert Whiskey

Christ climbed down
from His bare Tree
this year
and ran away to where
no fat handshaking stranger
in a red flannel suit
and a fake white beard
went around passing himself off
as some sort of North Pole saint
crossing the desert to Bethlehem
Pennsylvania
in a Volkswagon sled
drawn by rollicking Adirondack reindeer
with German names
and bearing sacks of Humble Gifts
from Saks Fifth Avenue
for everybody's imagined Christ child

Christ climbed down
from His bare Tree
this year
and ran away to where
no Bing Crosby carollers
groaned of a tight Christmas
and where no Radio City angels
iceskated wingless
thru a winter wonderland
into a jinglebell heaven
daily at 8:30
with Midnight Mass matinees

Christ climbed down
from His bare Tree
this year
and softly stole away into
some anonymous Mary's womb again
where in the darkest night
of everybody's anonymous soul
He awaits again
an unimaginable
and impossibly
Immaculate Reconception
the very craziest
of Second Comings

I AM WAITING

I am waiting for my case to come up
and I am waiting
for a rebirth of wonder
and I am waiting for someone
to really discover America
and wail
and I am waiting
for the discovery
of a new symbolic western frontier
and I am waiting
for the American Eagle
to really spread its wings
and straighten up and fly right
and I am waiting
for the Age of Anxiety
to drop dead
and I am waiting
for the war to be fought
which will make the world safe
for anarchy
and I am waiting
for the final withering away
of all governments

and I am perpetually awaiting
a rebirth of wonder

I am waiting for the Second Coming
and I am waiting
for a religious revival
to sweep thru the state of Arizona
and I am waiting
for the Grapes of Wrath to be stored
and I am waiting
for them to prove
that God is really American
and I am waiting
to see God on television
piped onto church altars
if only they can find
the right channel
to tune in on
and I am waiting
for the Last Supper to be served again
with a strange new appetizer
and I am perpetually awaiting
a rebirth of wonder

I am waiting for my number to be called
and I am waiting
for the living end
and I am waiting

for dad to come home
his pockets full
of irradiated silver dollars
and I am waiting
for the atomic tests to end
and I am waiting happily
for things to get much worse
before they improve
and I am waiting
for the Salvation Army to take over
and I am waiting
for the human crowd
to wander off a cliff somewhere
clutching its atomic umbrella
and I am waiting
for the meek to be blessed
and inherit the earth
without taxes
and I am waiting
for forests and animals
to reclaim the earth as theirs
and I am waiting
for a way to be devised
to destroy all nationalisms
without killing anybody
and I am waiting
for linnets and planets to fall like rain
and I am waiting for lovers and weepers

to lie down together again
in a new rebirth of wonder

I am waiting for the Great Divide to be crossed
and I am anxiously waiting
for the secret of eternal life to be discovered
by an obscure general practitioner
and save me forever from certain death
and I am waiting
for life to begin
and I am waiting
for the storms of life
to be over
and I am waiting
to set sail for happiness
and I am waiting
for a reconstructed Mayflower
to reach America
with its picture story and tv rights
sold in advance to the natives
and I am waiting
for the lost music to sound again
in the Lost Continent
in a new rebirth of wonder

I am waiting for the day
that maketh all things clear
and I am waiting

for Ole Man River
to just stop rolling along
past the country club
and I am waiting
for the deepest South
to just stop Reconstructing itself
in its own image
and I am waiting
for a sweet desegregated chariot
to swing low
and I am awaiting retribution
for what America did
to Tom Sawyer
and I am perpetually awaiting
a rebirth of wonder

I am waiting for Tom Swift to grow up
and I am waiting
for the American Boy
to take off Beauty's clothes
and get on top of her
and I am waiting
for Alice in Wonderland
to retransmit to me
her total dream of innocence
and I am waiting
for Childe Roland to come
to the final darkest tower

and I am waiting
for Aphrodite
to grow live arms
at a final disarmament conference
in a new rebirth of wonder

I am waiting
to get some intimations
of immortality
by recollecting my early childhood
and I am waiting
for the green mornings to come again
youth's dumb green fields come back again
and I am waiting
for some strains of unpremeditated art
to shake my typewriter
and I am waiting to write
the great indelible poem
and I am waiting
for the last long careless rapture
and I am perpetually waiting
for the fleeing lovers on the Grecian Urn
to catch each other up at last
and embrace
and I am awaiting
perpetually and forever
a renaissance of wonder

DOG

The dog trots freely in the street
and sees reality
and the things he sees
are bigger than himself
and the things he sees
are his reality
Drunks in doorways
Moons on trees
The dog trots freely thru the street
and the things he sees
are smaller than himself
Fish on newsprint
Ants in holes
Chickens in Chinatown windows
their heads a block away
The dog trots freely in the street
and the things he smells
smell something like himself
The dog trots freely in the street
past puddles and babies
cats and cigars
poolrooms and policemen
He doesn't hate cops
He merely has no use for them
and he goes past them

and past the dead cows hung up whole
in front of the San Francisco Meat Market
He would rather eat a tender cow
than a tough policeman
though either might do
And he goes past the Romeo Ravioli Factory
and past Coit's Tower
and past Congressman Doyle
He's afraid of Coit's Tower
but he's not afraid of Congressman Doyle
although what he hears is very discouraging
very depressing
very absurd
to a sad young dog like himself
to a serious dog like himself
But he has his own free world to live in
His own fleas to eat
He will not be muzzled
Congressman Doyle is just another
fire hydrant
to him
The dog trots freely in the street
and has his own dog's life to live
and to think about
and to reflect upon
touching and tasting and testing everything
investigating everything
without benefit of perjury
a real realist
with a real tale to tell

and a real tail to tell it with
a real live
            barking
                    democratic dog
engaged in real
                free enterprise
with something to say
                    about ontology
something to say
            about reality
                        and how to see it

                                and how to hear it
with his head cocked sideways
                        at streetcorners
as if he is just about to have
                    his picture taken
                                for Victor Records
                listening for
                        His Master's Voice
            and looking
                    like a living questionmark
                            into the
                            great gramaphone
                            of puzzling existence
        with its wondrous hollow horn
            which always seems
            just about to spout forth
                        some Victorious answer
                        to everything

NEW YORK—ALBANY

God i had forgotten how
the Hudson burns
in indian autumn
Saugerties
Coxsackie
fall away through
all those trees
The leaves die turning
falling fallen
falling into loam of dark
yellow into death
Disappearing
falling fallen falling
god god those
'pestilence-stricken multitudes'
rushed into the streets
blown all blasted
They are hurting them
with wood rakes
They are raking them
in great hills
They are burning them
lord lord

the leaves curl burning
the curled smoke gives up
to eternity
Never
never the same leaf turn again
the same leaves burn
lord lord
in a red field
a white stallion stands
and pees his oblivion
upon those leaves
washing my bus window
only now blacked out
by a covered bridge
we flash through
only once
No roundtrip ticket
Lord lord never returning
the youth years fallen
away back then
Under the Linden trees in Boston Common
Lord Lord
Trees think
through these woods of years
They flame forever
with those thoughts
Lord Lord
i did not see eternity

the other night
but now in burning
turning day
Lord Lord Lord
every bush burns
Love licks
all down
All gone
in the red end
Lord Lord Lord Lord
Small nuts fall
Mine too

UNDERWEAR

I didn't get much sleep last night
thinking about underwear
Have you ever stopped to consider
underwear in the abstract
When you really dig into it
some shocking problems are raised
Underwear is something
we all have to deal with
Everyone wears
some kind of underwear
Even Indians
wear underwear
Even Cubans
wear underwear
The Pope wears underwear I hope
Underwear is worn by Negroes
The Governor of Louisiana
wears underwear
I saw him on TV
He must have had tight underwear
He squirmed a lot
Underwear can really get you in a bind
Negroes often wear

white underwear
which may lead to trouble
You have seen the underwear ads
for men and women
so alike but so different
Women's underwear holds things up
Men's underwear holds things down
Underwear is one thing
men and women have in common
Underwear is all we have between us
You have seen the three-color pictures
with crotches encircled
to show the areas of extra strength
and three-way stretch
promising full freedom of action
Don't be deceived
It's all based on the two-party system
which doesn't allow much freedom of choice
the way things are set up
America in its Underwear
struggles thru the night
Underwear controls everything in the end
Take foundation garments for instance
They are really fascist forms
of underground government
making people believe
something but the truth
telling you what you can or can't do

Did you ever try to get around a girdle
Perhaps Non-Violent Action
is the only answer
Did Gandhi wear a girdle?
Did Lady Macbeth wear a girdle?
Was that why Macbeth murdered sleep?
And that spot she was always rubbing—
Was it really in her underwear?
Modern anglosaxon ladies
must have huge guilt complexes
always washing and washing and washing
Out damned spot—rub don't blot—
Underwear with spots very suspicious
Underwear with bulges very shocking
Underwear on clothesline a great flag of freedom
Someone has escaped his Underwear
May be naked somewhere
Help!
But don't worry
Everybody's still hung up in it
There won't be no real revolution
And poetry still the underwear of the soul
And underwear still covering
a multitude of faults
in the geological sense—
strange sedimentary stones, inscrutable cracks!
And that only the beginning
For does not the body stay alive

after death
and still need its underwear
or outgrow it
some organs said to reach full maturity
only after the head stops holding them back?
If I were you I'd keep aside
an oversize pair of winter underwear
Do not go naked into that good night
And in the meantime
keep calm and warm and dry
No use stirring ourselves up prematurely
'over Nothing'
Move forward with dignity
hand in vest
Don't get emotional
And death shall have no dominion
There's plenty of time my darling
Are we not still young and easy
Don't shout

TRUE CONFESSIONAL

I was conceived in the summer of Nineteen Eighteen
when some kind of war was going on
but it didn't stop two people
from making love in Ossining that year
I like to think on a riverbank in sun
on a picnic by the Hudson
as in a painting of the Hudson River School
or up at Bear Mountain maybe
after taking the old Hudson River Line
paddlewheel excursion steamer
(I may have added the paddlewheel—
the Hudson my Mississippi)
And on the way back she
already carried me
inside of her
I lawrence ferlinghetti
wrought from the dark in my mother long ago
born in a small back bedroom—
In the next room my brother heard
the first cry,
many years later wrote me—
"Poor Mom—No husband—No money—Pop dead—
How she went through it all—"

Someone squeezed my heart
to make it go
I cried and sprang up
Open eye open heart where
do I wander
into the heart of the world
Carried away
by another I knew not
And which of me shall know my brother?
'I am my son, my mother, my father,
I am born of myself
my own flesh sucked'
And someone squeezed my heart
to make me go
And I began to go
through my number
I was a wind-up toy
someone had dropped wound-up
into a world already
running down
The world had been going on
a long time already
but it made no difference
It was new it was like new
i made it new
i saw it shining
and it shone in the sun
and it spun in the sun

and the skein it spun
was pure light
My life was made of it
made of the skeins of light
The cobwebs of Night
were not on it
were not of it
It was too bright
to see
too luminous too numinous
to cast a shadow
and there was another world
behind the bright screens
I had only to close my eyes
for another world to appear
too near and too dear
to be anything but myself
my inside self
where everything real
was to happen
in this place which still exists
inside myself
and hasn't changed that much
certainly not as much
as the outside
with its bag of skin
and its 'aluminum beard'
and its blue blue eyes

which see as one eye
in the middle of the head
where everything happens
except what happens
in the heart
vajra lotus diamond heart
wherein I read
the poem that never ends

THOUGHTS TO A CONCERTO OF TELEMANN

'The curious upward stumbling motion
of the oboe d'amore'
must be love itself among the strands
of emotion. It is as if its motion
were not its own at all,
as if these hands
had never struck those strings
we sing to,
swing to
(as puppets do, unbroken)
as if we never really meant to
be so strung to
those sweet pitches
love so frets us to
so tautly
so mutely
(love's bodies laid like harps!)
and then as if
there never were still more
unspoken,
as if dumb mind did never grieve
among the woodwinds,
as if its chords

did never quiver anymore
as in a buried mandolin,
as if that love
were hardly in it
anymore,
nor sounded in it
anymore,
nor heart hear it
nor life bear it
anymore.
Yet it does, it does!

POUND AT SPOLETO

I walked into a loge in the Teatro Melisso, the lovely Renaissance salle where the poetry readings and the chamber concerts were held every day of the Spoleto Festival, and suddenly saw Ezra Pound for the first time, still as a mandarin statue in a box in a balcony at the back of the theatre, one tier up from the stalls. It was a shock, seeing only a striking old man in a curious pose, thin and long haired, aquiline at 80, head tilted strangely to one side, lost in permanent abstraction. . . . After three younger poets on stage, he was scheduled to read from his box, and there he sat with an old friend (who held his papers) waiting. He regarded the knuckles of his hands, moving them a very little, expressionless. Only once, when everyone else in the full theatre applauded someone on stage, did he rouse himself to clap, without looking up, as if stimulated by sound in a void. . . . After almost an hour, his turn came. Or after a life. . . . Everyone in the hall rose, turned and looked back and up at Pound in his booth, applauding. The applause was prolonged and Pound tried to rise from his armchair. A microphone was partly in the way. He grasped the arms of the chair with his boney hands and tried to rise. He could not and he tried again and could not. His old friend did not try to help him. Finally she put a poem in his hand, and after at least a minute his voice came out. First the jaw moved and then the voice came out, inaudible. A young Italian pulled the mike up very close to his face and held it there and the voice came over, frail but

64

stubborn, higher than I had expected, a thin, soft monotone. The hall had gone silent at a stroke. The voice knocked me down, so soft, so thin, so frail, so stubborn still. I put my head on my arms on the velvet sill of the box. I was surprised to see a single tear drop on my knee. The thin, indomitable voice went on. I went blind from the box, through the back door of it, into the empty corridor of the theatre where they still sat turned to him, went down and out, into the sunlight, weeping. . . .

Up above the town
                    by the ancient aqueduct
      the chestnut trees
                         were still in bloom
Mute birds
           flew in the valley
                              far below
      The sun shone
                    on the chestnut trees
and the leaves
              turned in the sun
           and turned and turned and turned
           And would continue turning
His voice
          went on
               and on
                      through the leaves. . . .

RECIPE FOR HAPPINESS IN KHABAROVSK
OR ANYPLACE

One grand boulevard with trees
with one grand café in sun
with strong black coffee in very small cups

One not necessarily very beautiful
man or woman who loves you

One fine day

BASEBALL CANTO

Watching baseball
sitting in the sun
eating popcorn
reading Ezra Pound
and wishing Juan Marichal
would hit a hole right through
the Anglo-Saxon tradition
in the First Canto
and demolish the barbarian invaders
When the San Francisco Giants take the field
and everybody stands up to the National Anthem
with some Irish tenor's voice
piped over the loudspeakers
with all the players struck dead in their places
and the white umpires like Irish cops
in their black suits and little black caps
pressed over their hearts
standing straight and still
like at some funeral of a blarney bartender
and all facing East
as if expecting some Great White Hope
or the Founding Fathers
to appear on the horizon

like 1066 or 1776 or all that
But Willie Mays appears instead
in the bottom of the first
and a roar goes up
      as he clouts the first one into the sun
          and takes off
             like a footrunner from Thebes
      The ball is lost in the sun
          and maidens wail after him
            but he keeps running
              through the Anglo-Saxon epic
And Tito Fuentes comes up
    looking like a bullfighter
    in his tight pants and small pointed shoes

And the rightfield bleachers go mad
    with chicanos & blacks & Brooklyn beerdrinkers
      "Sweet Tito! Sock it to heem, Sweet Tito!"
And Sweet Tito puts his foot in the bucket
      and smacks one that don't come back at all
      and flees around the bases
  like he's escaping from the United Fruit Company
  as the gringo dollar beats out the Pound
      and Sweet Tito beats it out
      like he's beating out usury
      not to mention fascism and anti-semitism
And Juan Marichal comes up
  and the chicano bleachers go loco again

as Juan belts the first fast ball
            out of sight
                  and rounds first and keeps going
            and rounds second and rounds third
                              and keeps going
                              and hits pay-dirt
            to the roars of the grungy populace
As some nut presses the backstage panic button
for the tape-recorded National Anthem again
to save the situation
but it don't stop nobody this time
in their revolution round the loaded white bases
in this last of the great Anglo-Saxon epics
in the *Territorio Libre* of baseball

JACK OF HEARTS
(for Bob Dylan)

Who are we now, who are we ever,
Skin books parchment bodies libraries of the living
gilt almanacs of the very rich
encyclopedias of little people
packs of players face down
on faded maps of America
with no Jack of Hearts
in the time of the ostrich
Fields full of rooks
dumb pawns in black-and-white kingdoms
And revolutions the festivals of the oppressed
and festivals the little revolutions
of the bourgeoisie
where gypsy fortune tellers deal
without the Jack of Hearts
the black-eyed one who sees all ways
the one with the eye of a horse
the one with the lights in his eye
the one with his eye on the star named Nova
the one for the ones with no one to lead them
the one whose day has just begun
the one with the star in his cap

the cat with future feet
looking like a Jack of Hearts
mystic Jack Zen Jack with crazy koans
Vegas Jack who rolls the bones
the high roller behind the dealer
the one who'll shake them
the one who'll shake the ones unshaken
the fearless one
the one without bullshit
the stud with the straightest answer
the one with blazing words for guns
the distance runner with the word to pass
the night rider with the urgent message
The man from La Mancha riding bareback
The one who bears the great tradition
and breaks it
The Mysterious Stranger who comes & goes
The Jack of Hearts who speaks out
the one who sees what the ostrich sees in the sand
the one who digs the mystery
and stands on the corner smiling
at the ones who don't want to look
at what's going down around them
the shut-eye ones who wish
that someone else would seize the day
that someone else would tell them
which way up and which way out
and whom to hate and whom to love

Saint Jack who had the Revelations
and spoke the poem of apocalypse
Poet Jack with the light pack
who travels by himself
and leave the ladies smiling
Dharma Jack with the beatitudes
drunk on a bus addressing everyone
the silent ones with the frozen faces
who never speak to strangers
the one who heals the Hamlet in them
the silent Ham who never acts
like the Jack of Hearts
the dude on the corner in two-tone shoes
who knows the name of the game
the kid who paints the fence
the boy who digs the treasure up
the boy with the beans on the beanstalk
the dandy man the candy man
the one with the lollipops
the harlequin man
in front of the house that Jack built
where sleeps the Cock that crowed in the morn
where sleeps the Cow with the crumpled horn
where sleeps the dude who kept the horse
with the beautiful form
and kissed the Maiden all forlorn
the Jack of the pack all tattered and torn
the one the queen keeps her eye on
Dark Rider on a white horse

Prophet stoned on the wheel of fortune
Sweet singer with harp half-hid
who speaks with the cry of cicadas
the true tale of sound and fury
the Jack of Hearts who lays it out
who tells it as it is
the one who wears no watch
yet tells the time too truly
the one who tells his dream
the black dream the white dream
of the Jack of Hearts
whose skeleton is neither black nor white
the long dream the dream of heads & hearts
that turns the Hanged Man right side up
and saves the Drowned Sailor
the wet dream the hard dream the sweet dream
of the Deck Hand on the tall ship sailing softly
Blackjack yellowjack the steeplejack
who sets the clock in the tower
and sees the chimes of freedom flashing
and finds the sun-stone of himself
the woman-man
the whole man
who holds all worlds together
when all is said and all is done
in the wild eye the wide eye
of the Jack of Hearts
who stands in a doorway
clothed in sun

PEOPLE GETTING DIVORCED

People getting divorced
        riding around with their clothes in the car
    and wondering what happened
                    to everyone and everything
                        including their other
                                pair of shoes
        And if you spy one
            then who knows what happened
                        to the other
                        with tongue alack
    and years later not even knowing
                    if the other ever
                            found a mate
                        without splitting the seams
                        or remained intact
                                unlaced
    and the sole
            ah the soul
                    a curious conception
        hanging on somehow
                        to walk again
                            in the free air
                    once the heel
                            has been replaced

OLBERS' PARADOX

And I heard the learned astronomer
                  whose name was Heinrich Olbers
speaking to us across the centuries
    about how he observed with naked eye
        how in the sky there were
              some few stars close up
and the further away he looked
             the more of them there were
with infinite numbers of clusters of stars
      in myriad Milky Ways & myriad nebulae

So that from this we may deduce
      that in the infinite distances
             there must be a place
                there *must* be a place
                   where all is light
and that the light from that high place
                   where all is light
        simply hasn't got here yet
        which is why we still have night

But when at last that light arrives
    when at last it does get here

the part of day we now call Night
will have a white sky
with little black dots in it
little black holes
where once were stars

And then in that symbolic
so poetic place
which will be ours
we'll be our own true shadows
and our own illumination
on a sunset earth

DEEP CHESS

Life itself like championship chess
                          dark players jousting
              on a checkered field
                          where you have only
              so much time
                          to complete your moves
And your clock running
                          all the time
          and if you take
                          too much time
                                      for one move
              you have that much less
                                      for the rest
                          of your life
And your opponent
                          dark or fair
              (which may or may not be
                                      life itself)
bugging you with his deep eyes
   or obscenely wiggling his crazy eyebrows
      or blowing smoke in your face
         or crossing and recrossing his legs
                                      or her legs

or otherwise screwing around
and acting like some insolent invulnerable
unbeatable god
who can read your mind & heart
And one hasty move
may ruin you
for you must play
deep chess
(like the one deep game Spassky won from Fischer)
And if your unstudied opening
was not too brilliant
you must play to win not draw
and suddenly come up with
a new Nabokov variation
And then lay Him out at last
with some super end-game
no one has ever even dreamed of

And there's still time—
Your move

THE GENERAL SONG OF HUMANITY

On the coast of Chile where Neruda lived
   it's well known that
      seabirds often steal
            letters out of mailboxes
               which they would like to scan
               for various reasons
Shall I enumerate the reasons?
     They are quite clear
         even given the silence of birds
                  on the subject
       (except when they speak of it
              among themselves
               between cries)
First of all
       they steal the letters because
           they sense that the General Song
              of the words of everyone
          hidden in these letters
     must certainly bear the keys
       to the heart itself of humanity
           which the birds themselves
              have never been able to fathom
          (in fact entertaining much doubt

that there actually are
                        hearts in humans)
And then these birds have a further feeling
            that their own general song
                    might somehow be enriched
                            by these strange cries of humans
            (What a weird bird-brain idea
                that our titterings might enlighten them)
But when they stole away
                with Neruda's own letters
                out of his mailbox at Isla Negra
            they were in fact stealing back
                            their own Canto General
                which he had originally gathered
                                    from them
                with their omnivorous & ecstatic
                                sweeping vision
    But now that Neruda is dead
        no more such letters are written
        and they must play it by ear again—
            the high great song
                        in the heart of our blood & silence

CUERNAVACA, OCTOBER 26 '75

ROUGH SONG OF ANIMALS DYING

In a dream within a dream I dreamt a dream
of the reality of existence
inside the ultimate computer
which is the universe
in which the Arrow of Time
flies both ways
through bent space
In a dream within a dream I dreamt a dream
of all the animals dying
the wild animals the longhaired animals
winged animals feathered animals
clawed & scaled & furry animals
rutting & dying & dying
In a dream within a dream I dreamt a dream
of creatures everywhere dying out
in shrinking rainforests
in piney woods & high sierras
on shrinking prairies & tumbleweed mesas
captured beaten strapped starved & stunned
cornered & traded
species not meant to be nomadic
wandering rootless as man
In a dream within a dream I dreamt a dream

of all the animals crying out
in their hidden places
slinking away & crawling about
through the last wild places
through the dense underbrush
the last Great Thickets
beyond the mountains
crisscrossed with switchbacks
beyond the marshes
beyond the plains & fences
(the West won with barbed-wire machines)
in the high country
in the low country
crisscrossed with highways
In a dream within a dream I dreamt a dream
of how they feed & rut & run & hide
In a dream within a dream I saw
how the seals are beaten on the ice-fields
the soft white furry seals with eggshell skulls
the Great Green turtles beaten & eaten
exotic birds netted & caged & tethered
rare wild beasts & strange reptiles & weird woozoos
hunted down for zoos
by bearded blackmarketeers
who afterwards ride around Singapore
in German limousines
In a dream within a dream I dreamt a dream
of the earth heating up & drying out

under its canopy of carbon monoxide
breathed out by a billion
infernal combustion engines
mixed with the sweet smell of burning flesh
In a dream within a dream I dreamt a dream
of animals calling to each other
in codes we never understand
The seal and steer cry out
in the same voice
as they are clubbed
in stockyards & snowfields
The wounds never heal
in the commonweal of animals
We steal their lives
to feed our own
and with their lives
our dreams are sown
In a dream within a dream I dreamt a dream
of the daily scrimmage for existence
in the wind-up model of the universe
the spinning meat-wheel world
in which I was a fish who eats his tail
in which I was a claw upon a beach
in which I was a snake upon a tree
in which I was a serpent's egg
a yin-yang yolk of good and evil
about to consume itself

WHITE ON WHITE

Today I'll write white on white
wear nothing but white
drink nothing but white
eat nothing but white
And I would be that sea-creature
who eats light
straining the ocean for its phosphorous
For present time
is a 'white dot' space
and white is the sand
in the hourglass
running out
White dunes of Africa
running through it
Snows of Siberia
sifting through it
The seas white with sperm
under the white moon
where aluminum stars wheel about
noiselessly
over quivering meat-wheel earth
with its white wales
white phagocytes

white bleached skulls
and albino animals
(Blacks bleached out
into white men?)
And to dream of white string
a symbol of innocence
Though the color of death be white
And the world checkered with death
white-on-black & black-on-white
"dumb pawns
in black-and-white kingdoms"
And angel stands on a station platform
slowly shaking its gossamer wings
A white horse
comes alone from a torn village
Everywhere around the earth
on station platforms they
are still putting up the placards
No pasarán
Go back Wrong way
White searchlights
search the sky
The gun turrets turn
on the old Walls
The angel slowly moves its wings
breathing the light white air
The earth breathes and trembles with it
The governed

will be governed
Liberty is not freedom
Eros versus civilization
No Way
without a pass
It is snowing white documents
The very rich
get richer still
A white gloved hand
still reaches out the window
for the money in the cup
Liberty is not free
Some poor still ride some trains
The angel
stands on the edge
of the station platform
slowly moving its large white wings
which look too fragile
to lift the body of being
which still breathes anarchist air
And the train
the train made of nothing but boxcars
jammed with three billion people
still standing in the station
trembling

(AFTER READING BREYTEN BREYTENBACH,
IMPRISONED AFRIKAANS WHITE POET)

THE OLD ITALIANS DYING

For years the old Italians have been dying
all over America
For years the old Italians in faded felt hats
have been sunning themselves and dying
You have seen them on the benches
in the park in Washington Square
the old Italians in their black high button shoes
the old men in their old felt fedoras
                with stained hatbands
have been dying and dying
          day by day
You have seen them
every day in Washington Square San Francisco
the slow bell
tolls in the morning
in the Church of Peter & Paul
in the marzipan church on the plaza
toward ten in the morning the slow bell tolls
in the towers of Peter & Paul
and the old men who are still alive
sit sunning themselves in a row
on the wood benches in the park
and watch the processions in and out

funerals in the morning
weddings in the afternoon
slow bell in the morning Fast bell at noon
In one door out the other
the old men sit there in their hats
and watch the coming & going
You have seen them
the ones who feed the pigeons
                cutting the stale bread
                    with their thumbs & penknives
the ones with old pocketwatches
the old ones with gnarled hands
                            and wild eyebrows
the ones with the baggy pants
                        with both belt & suspenders
the grappa drinkers with teeth like corn
the Piemontesi the Genovesi the Siciliani
                smelling of garlic & pepperoni
the ones who loved Mussolini
the old fascists
the ones who loved Garibaldi
the old anarchists reading *L'Umanita Nuova*
the ones who loved Sacco & Vanzetti
They are almost all gone now
They are sitting and waiting their turn
and sunning themselves in front of the church
over the doors of which is inscribed
a phrase which would seem to be unfinished

from Dante's *Paradiso*
about the glory of the One
                                who moves everything . . .
The old men are waiting
for it to be finished
for their glorious sentence on earth
                                to be finished
the slow bell tolls & tolls
the pigeons strut about
not even thinking of flying
the air too heavy with heavy tolling
The black hired hearses draw up
the black limousines with black windowshades
shielding the widows
the widows with the long black veils
who will outlive them all
You have seen them
madre di terra, madre di mare
The widows climb out of the limousines
The family mourners step out in stiff suits
The widows walk so slowly
up the steps of the cathedral
fishnet veils drawn down
leaning hard on darkcloth arms
Their faces do not fall apart
They are merely drawn apart
They are still the matriarchs
outliving everyone

the old dagos dying out
in Little Italys all over America
the old dead dagos
hauled out in the morning sun
that does not mourn for anyone
One by one Year by year
they are carried out
The bell
never stops tolling
The old Italians with lapstrake faces
are hauled out of the hearses
by the paid pallbearers
in mafioso mourning coats & dark glasses
The old dead men are hauled out
in their black coffins like small skiffs
They enter the true church
for the first time in many years
in these carved black boats
     ready to be ferried over
The priests scurry about
    as if to cast off the lines
The other old men
      still alive on the benches
watch it all with their hats on
You have seen them sitting there
waiting for the bocce ball to stop rolling
waiting for the bell
     to stop tolling & tolling

for the slow bell
                    to be finished tolling
telling the unfinished *Paradiso* story
as seen in an unfinished phrase
                    on the face of a church
as seen in a fisherman's face
in a black boat without sails
making his final haul

TWO SCAVENGERS IN A TRUCK, TWO
BEAUTIFUL PEOPLE IN A MERCEDES

At the stoplight waiting for the light
                    Nine A.M. downtown San Francisco
  a bright yellow garbage truck
                with two garbagemen in red plastic blazers
  standing on the back stoop
                    one on each side hanging on
  and looking down into
                    an elegant open Mercedes
      with an elegant couple in it
The man
      in a hip three-piece linen suit
        with shoulder-length blond hair & sunglasses
The young blond woman so casually coifed
                with a short skirt and colored stockings
  on the way to his architect's office

And the two scavengers up since Four A.M.
                        grungy from their route
            on the way home
The older of the two with grey iron hair
                        and hunched back

looking down like some
                              gargoyle Quasimodo
And the younger of the two
                        also with sunglasses & longhair
    about the same age as the Mercedes driver

And both scavengers gazing down
                              as from a great distance
            at the cool couple
    as if they were watching some odorless TV ad
                    in which everything is always possible
And the very red light for an instant
                holding all four close together
        as if anything at all were possible
                              between them
        across that small gulf
                    in the high seas
                              of this democracy

from PARIS TRANSFORMATIONS

Clay somnambule returned
                              after many years away
        walking and walking
                              through once-loved Paris
    Gare du Nord to Montparnasse
        Rue de la Roquette and Place Voltaire
            Place Léon Blum and Père Lachaise
                Les Halles and Tour St. Jacques
                    Saint Sulpice and Cherche Midi
                    (where I searched my Noon)

Strode through the streets
                thirsty and sad
                              (yet exultant!)
                carrying nothing
                              but youth

Now the closed bus carries me
                past the place I lay on the quai

The map of Paris
                stamped upon my brainpan

* * *

The white sun of Paris
softens sidewalks
sketches white shadows on skylights
traps a black cat
on a distant balcony

And the whole city sleeping drifts
through white space
like a lost dirigible
unconscious of
the immense mystery

* * *

Tristes banlieues,
saisons, châteaux,
et toutes ces tristesses
de la Ligne de Sceaux.
But then again the things that still amaze
And autumn capitols
their avenues of leaves ablaze
avec leurs douces fugues,
tristes banlieues,
saisons, châteaux,
et toutes ses tristes joies
qui oun lieu
au coeur brisé.

* * *

For years I never thought of death.
Now the breath
of the eternal harlequin
makes me look up
as if a defrocked Someone were there
who might make me into an angel
playing piano on a riverboat.

HE WITH THE BEATING WINGS

The lark has no tree
                    the crow no roost
  the owl no setting place
              the nightingale
                            no certain song
And he with the beating wings
                no place to light
                    in the neon dawn
            his tongue too long ago
                      retuned
      by those ornithologists
                  the state has hired
    to make sure
          the bird population of the world
    remains stable
             and pinioned
There is no need
      to clip its claws
Its tongue will do
         Tether the tongue
  and all falls fallow
      The wild seed drops
           into nothingness

Tether the tongue
     and all falls
          into silence
a condition ever desired
          by tyrants
     not least of which is
          the great state
with its benevolent birdwatchers
          with their nets and binoculars
watching out for
     the wild one
He that bears Eros
          like a fainting body
     He that hears
          the gold bough

He
     with the beating wings

PLAN DU CENTRE DE PARIS À VOL D'OISEAU

Flying away to Milan
I look down and back at Paris
(as in that famous map
seen by a bird in flight)
and think of Allen yesterday
saying it was all 'solidified nostalgia'—
houses monuments and streets
bare trees and parks down there
fixed in time (and the time is forever)
exactly where we left them years ago
our bodies passed through them
as through a transparent scrim
Early versions of ourselves
transmuted now
two decades later
And was that myself
standing on that far corner
Place Saint-Sulpice
first arrived in Paris—
seabag slung—
(fancying myself some seaborn Conrad
carrying Coleridge's albatross?)
or was that myself walking

through the Tuileries in early snow?
And here Danton met Robespierre
(both later to descend into earth
through that Metro entrance)
And here Sartre lived with Beauvoir
above the Café Bonaparte
before death
shook them apart
(The myth goes on)
And here in the Luxembourg
I sat by a balustrade
in a rented iron chair
reading Proust and Apollinaire
while the day turned to dust
and a nightwood sprang up around me
Solidified nostalgia indeed—
the smell of Gaulois still hangs in the air
And in the cemetery of Père Lachaise
the great stone tombs still yawn
with the solidified ennui of eternity
And, yes, here I knew such aloneness—
at the corner of another street
the dawn yawned
in some trauma I was living in back then
Paris itself a floating dream
a great stone ship adrift
made of dusk and dawn and darkness—
dumb trauma

of youth!
such wastes of love
such wordless hungers
mute neuroses
yearnings & gropings
fantasies & flame-outs
such endless walking
through the bent streets
such fumbling art
(models drawn with blindfolds)
such highs and sweet inebriations—
I salute you now
dumb inchoate youth
(callow stripling!)
and offer you my left hand
with a slight derisive laugh

EXPRESSIONIST HISTORY OF GERMAN EXPRESSIONISM

The Blue Rider rode over The Bridge into the Bauhaus
on more than one blue horse
Franz Marc made his blue mark
on the blue scene
And Kirchner cantered through the dark circus
on a different dark horse
Emil Nolde never moldy danced boldly
around a golden calf
Max Pechstein fished in river landscapes
and fooled around with his models
(They all did that)
Rottluff painted his rusty lust
and Otto Mueller ate cruellers
as his painting got cruder
Erich Heckel heckled himself with madmen
and thereby foresaw their mad ends
Norwegian Munch let out a silent scream
Jawlensky made Matisse look mad and Russian
And Kandinsky grew insanely
incandescent
Kokoschka drew his own *sturm und drang*
Käthe Kollwitz chalked the face

of Death and the Mother
Schwitters twittered through trash cities
and Klee became a clay mobile
swaying to the strains of the Blue Angel
Otto Dix drew a dying warrior
on his steely palette
Grosz glimpsed the grossest
in the gathering storm
Max Beckmann saw the sinking of the Titanic
and Meidner painted the Apocalypse
Feininger traced a Tragic Being
and fingered skyscrapers
which fell across the Atlantic
(and the Bauhaus in its final antic
fell on Chicago)
Meanwhile back in Berlin
Hitler was painting himself
into a corner
And his ovens were heating
as a Tin Drum began heating

THE PHOTO OF EMILY

She wore a cloche hat
She was Aunt Emily
She spoke French She had a job
as a French governess
She stood on the bridge in Bronxville
over the Bronx River the little river
with its little woods and the little bridge
and the swimming hole and the woods
where we played Robin Hood
I thought I was Robin Hood
or one of his deerskin men
I wanted a deerskin suit
more than anything
I remember that clearly when I was eight
I stayed awake at night
thinking how to make it how to get it
I would have robbed a rich traveller
(That's how rebels arc born)
She stood on the bridge in her hat
I came to her from the woods
where I'd been playing
by the little brown river
with its dirty crayfish

I came up to her
in her long lace dress and black pumps
She had elegant feet
long feet
an 'aristocrat's' she would say
She was a bit mad and elegant
Even then I knew it
She was Catholic in a mad way
as if she had some special personal connection
with the Pope
She thought of herself as a writer
as having something special to say
in French
I thought of her as my French mother
She was my mother's French sister
the sister who'd been born in France
the family so mixed up
between Portugal and France
and the Virgin Islands
which was the route my mother's family took
to the United States
and Coney Island where the French kept
boardinghouses
and where my mother met my father
when he came from Lombardy
speaking only Lombard
and ended up the first night
in that boardinghouse at Coney

My French mother Emily stands on the bridge
in the old photo
the only photo I had of her
A dark bridge and her face in shadow
Or perhaps her face was light once
and the photo darkened
There is a pearly strangeness
in the dark light
It is all I have of her
She must have had a box camera that day
I was wearing short pants
on that little stone bridge
(And who took the picture
of the two of us together
arms around each other?
So silent the old picture—
If it could only speak!)
It is her day off in the Nineteen Twenties
I am nine—
Where now
that elegant cloche hat
that woman lost in time
a shadowy strangeness is all
She had fine skin
gossamer hair
cut like Garbo
or Louise Brooks
but not so beautiful

She had a wen on her breast
Might I not find that hat
and that woman still—
a seamstress in the back
of some small thrift shop—
Come back, come back—
At least the photo
might I not at least
find the photo again
in some lost album
with black cardboard pages
there's the photo
held on the stiff page
by little paper triangles pasted on
the photo of Emily
mad and elegant
thinking herself a great writer
with something to say to the world
in her shadow hat
having her picture taken
with the child she always wanted
She had lovers but no child
She stood by the bedside and took me
Life went on with us
The photo darkened
She was too distracted
too gypsy-like too self-willed
too obsessed too

passionately articulate
burning too bright
too much a lunatic of loving
to keep that child
who ran off finally
into the dark park of those days
by the Bronx River
and sees her now
nowhere else in memory
except by that dark bridge
And saw her never again
And never saw her again
except in the back of old boutiques
peered into now again
with haunting glance
in the Rue de Seine

THE REBELS

Star-stricken still
          we lie under them
                  in dome of night
     as they wheel about
            in their revolutions
    forming and reforming
                (oh not for us!)
        their splendiferous
           phosphor fabrications

Ah the wheelwright of it
               (whoever he or she or it)
    chief fabricator
          of the night of it
     of the night to set it in
           this cut-glass
             diamond diagram

Upstairs
    in the lighted attic
       under the burning eaves
             of time

lamps hung out
           (to guide far more far-out voyagers
                    than ourselves)

Still antic stars
           shoot out
                    burst out—
                               errant rebels
                    even there
           in the perfect pattern
                    of some utopia
           shooting up
                    tearing the
                               silver web
           of perfect symmetry

As in a palm of hand
           the perfect plan of line
                    of life and heart and head
      struck across of a sudden
                    by one
                               cataclysmic tear

Yet all not asunder
           all not lost to darkness
      all held together still
                    at some still center
           even now

in the almost incendiary dawn
as still another
rebel burning bright
strikes its match upon
our night

ROMAN MORN

Ah these sweet Roman mornings—
    I open the shutters
         high above the back courtyard
   and look out over the
            silent roofs . . .
     the air still cool . . .
        no birds on the tile chimneys . . .
   shutters still shut across the way . . .
      a windless weathervane far off . . .
      a whistle in the street below . . .
Now there's a pigeon
        flutters a wing in an eave
      on terracotta tilings
Ah now a white dove
        alights on a cupola
  as first sun slants through
The sun
    floods over
          Shadows stretch out
           on rooftop gardens
There is a sweetness in the air
    The silent dove turns about
        on the bent tiles

They are opening the shutters
    on the back side
        of the Palazzo Farnese
  A phrase of French floats up
          sounding alien
Somewhere a woman starts to sing
          a snatch of opera
Somewhere an angelus starts to ring
Somewhere a woman shouts *Angelo, Angelo!*
Somewhere he washes off his sins
The day begins and begins

BELATED PALINODE FOR DYLAN THOMAS

In Wales at Laugharne at last I stand beside
  his cliff-perched writing shed
    above the coursing waters
      where the hawk hangs still
        above the cockle-strewn shingle
Where he walked in a glory of all his days
    (before the weather turned around)
And *aie! aie!* a waterbird far away
    cries and cries again
      over St. Johns Hill
And in his tilted boathouse now
    a tape of himself is playing—
      his lush voice
        his plush voice
          his posh accent
            (too BBC-fulsome, cried the Welsh)
              now echoes through his little
                upstairs room
And *aie! aie!*
  echo the waterbirds once again
Beyond his sounding shed
    a fig tree hides the sea
      A fishboat heeled over

a grebe afloat far out
a coracle abandoned
a rusted coaler out of Cardiff still
a bold green headland lost in sun
Beyond which lie (across an ocean and a continent)
San Francisco's white wood houses
and a poet's sun-bleached cottage
on Bolinas' far lagoon
with its wind-torn Little Mesa
(so very like St. Johns Hill)
A single kestrel soars over
riding the salt wind
'high tide and the heron's call'
still echoing
(Aie! aie! it calls and calls again)
As in his listing boathouse now
his great recorded voice runs out
(grave as a gravedigger in his grave)
leaving a sounding void of light
for poets and herons to fill
(Drowned down in New York's White Horse Tavern
he went not gentle into his good night)
And Far West poets calling still
over St. Johns Hill
to the loveliest poet of all our days
sweet singer of Swansea
lushed singer of Laugharne
Dylan of all our days

Driving a cardboard automobile without a license
                    at the turn of the century
        my father ran into my mother
                            on a fun-ride at Coney Island
            having spied each other eating
                        in a French boardinghouse nearby
And having decided right there and then
                        that she was for him entirely
        he followed her into
                        the playland of that evening
        where the headlong meeting
                        of their ephemeral flesh on wheels
            hurtled them forever together

And I now in the back seat
                    of their eternity
                        reaching out to embrace them

                    * * *

116

And Pablo Neruda
        that Chilean omnivore of poetry
        who wanted to
                put everything in
                   and take nothing out
                     (of his *Canto General)*
      said to me in Havana Libre Hilton 1959
               'I love your wide open poetry'
        by which he meant a certain kind of
            poesía norteamericana
                and its rebel band who
               rose over the rooftops of
                    tenement boneyards
               intent on making out
And made out of madness
        a hundred years of beatitude

'So boring I'm snoring'
            cried Joe Public
           before *they* came along
        and busted out the sides
              of *Poetry* Chicago
        and various New Yorkerish
               poetasters
            out of their Westchester cradles
                    endlessly rocking
           on the Times Square Shuttle
        between the *Times Book Review*

                                         and the Algonquin
                       while lady critics and gent professors
                                    moaned about poetic pederasts
                                                    at Columbia

They cruised Times Square and America
                            and cruised into history
                          'waving genitals and manuscripts'
And tuned their holy unholy voices
                     to a wide open society
                                that didn't yet exist

And so jump-started
                  the stalled merry-go-round
                                        of American ecstasy
                              left along East River's
                                         echoing shores
                         after Old Walt stepped off
                                         Brooklyn Ferry
                                         into the heart of America

                                * * *

O

heart

involuntary muscle

O

heart

mute lover

without a tongue

of your own

I would speak for you

whenever you

(seeing a certain someone)

feel love

* * *

Oh you gatherer
     of the fine ash of poetry
        ash of the too-white flame
               of poetry

Consider those who have burned before you
                  in the so-white fire

Crucible of Keats and Campana
     Bruno and Sappho
           Rimbaud and Poe and Corso
      And Shelley burning on the beach
             at Viarreggio

And now in the night
     in the general conflagration
       the white light
          still consuming us
      small clowns
        with our little tapers
          held to the flame

* * *

The Green Street Mortuary Marching Band
                marches right down Green Street
                        and turns into Columbus Avenue
                            where all the café sitters at
                                    the sidewalk café tables
                                        sit talking and laughing and
                                            looking right through it
        as if it happened every day in
            little old wooden North Beach San Francisco
                but at the same time feeling thrilled
                    by the stirring sound of the gallant marching band
                        as if it were celebrating life and
                                                never heard of death

And right behind it comes the open hearse
        with the closed casket and the
                    big framed picture under glass propped up
                        showing the patriarch who
                                            has just croaked
And now all seven members of
        the Green Street Mortuary Marching Band
            with the faded gold braid on their
                                    beat-up captains' hats
                        raise their bent axes and
                        start blowing all more or less
                                            together and

out comes this Onward Christian Soldiers like
            you heard it once upon a time only
                    much slower with a dead beat

And now you see all the relatives behind the
            closed glass windows of the long black cars and
                    their faces are all shiny like they
                        been weeping with washcloths and
                            all super serious
                    like as if the bottom has just dropped out of
                            their private markets and
            there's the widow all in weeds, and the sister with the
bent frame and the mad brother who never got through school and
Uncle Louie with the wig and there they all are assembled together
and facing each other maybe for the first time in a long time but their
masks and public faces are all in place as they face outward behind
the traveling corpse up ahead and oompah oompah goes the band
very slow with the trombones and the tuba and the trumpets and the
big bass drum and the corpse hears nothing or everything and it's a
glorious autumn day in old North Beach if only he could have lived
to see it Only we wouldn't have had the band who half an hour later
can be seen straggling back silent along the sidewalks looking like
hungover brokendown Irish bartenders dying for a drink or a last
hurrah

THE CHANGING LIGHT

The changing light at San Francisco
                    is none of your East Coast light
                            none of your
                                        pearly light of Paris
The light of San Francisco
                        is a sea light
                                    an island light
And the light of fog
                    blanketing the hills
            drifting in at night
                        through the Golden Gate
                                to lie on the city at dawn
And then the halcyon late mornings
            after the fog burns off
            and the sun paints white houses
                            with the sea light of Greece
                    with sharp clean shadows
                    making the town look like
                            it had just been painted
But the wind comes up at four o'clock
                                    sweeping the hills
And then the veil of light of early evening
And then another scrim

when the new night fog
                        floats in
And in that vale of light
                the city drifts
                        anchorless upon the ocean

YACHTS IN SUN

The yachts the white yachts
    with their white sails in sunlight
                catching the wind and
                        heeling over
All together racing now
                for the white buoy
      to tack about
        to come about beyond it
And then come running in
      before the spanking wind
        white spinnakers billowing
           off Fort Mason San Francisco
Where once drowned down
      an Alcatraz con escaping
        whose bones today are sand
                fifty fathoms down
        still imprisoned now
                in the glass of the sea
As the so skillful yachts
        freely pass over

DICTIONARIES OF LIGHT

The sun the sun
                comes round the corner
                    like a shining knight of old
                        galloping over the landscape
                                on the horses of morning
            And shaking his lance over us
                in trance of night
                    awakens us to speak or sing
                                to banish death and darkness
And each steed a word
                each verb a stallion
                    reared up against all ignorance
Untamed rampant radicals
                        in dictionaries of light

from SURREAL MIGRATIONS

Rain is falling on a mirror made of sunshine
Absinthe lover full of absence
your eyes elsewhere
      your hyacinth hair
                    your naiad air
   your fine nude legs in sun
In olde Europa
Proust and his madeleine
Apollinaire's migraine
Afternoons on the Grande Jatte
The arrogance of André Breton
Little Addie the Housepainter
with the toothbrush moustache
Is Paris burning?
The Valkyries were singing
unter den linden
Lilli Marlene Lilli Marlene
Underneath the lamplight
by the village green
I must arise and go now
We'll find a place away
morning sun with leaves
full upon you

dappled darling
the very idea of love
Heart shot through with holes
a rain of crystal
a loud silence
a far-off singing
Some heard the silence of the sea
Some drank Vichy
Some were shot running
Some were shot against a wall
Some burned singing
Sun eternal firework
Sun the only god remaining
The moon a crystal mirror
                         eternal deceiver
Is love still burning
      Do lovers alone wear sunlight?
Dica darling
                 tell me tell me
Love lie with me
                 beyond the sea
The quays black with voyagers
A crowd flows over London Bridge
Hurry up please
Lady Liberty with flaming torch
stands upon her little island
having dropped her French accent
Don't give me your homeless

Jetliners land
without folding their wings
In a dense fog the foghorns
still are sounding
At Ambrose Light the great ships
still grope through it
Dica darling
A crowd flows over Brooklyn Bridge
Hey taxi!

THE LORD'S LAST PRAYER

Our father whose art's in heaven
Hollow be thy name
Unless things change
Thy kingdom come and gone
Thy will will be undone
On earth as it isn't heaven
Give us this day our daily bread
At least three times a day
And lead us not into temptation
too often on weekdays
But deliver us from evil
Whose presence remains unexplained
In thy kingdom of power and glory
Ah, Man!

HISTORY OF THE AIRPLANE

(Music: U.S. National Anthem at half speed)

And the Wright brothers said they thought they had invented
something that could make peace on earth (if the wrong brothers
didn't get hold of it) when their wonderful flying machine took off
at Kitty Hawk into the kingdom of birds but the parliament of birds
was freaked out by this man-made bird and fled to heaven

And then the famous Spirit of Saint Louis took off eastward and
flew across the Big Pond with Lindy at the controls in his leather
helmet and goggles hoping to sight the doves of peace but he did
not Even though he circled Versailles

And then the famous Yankee Clipper took off in the opposite
direction and flew across the terrific Pacific but the pacific doves
were frightened by this strange amphibious bird and hid in the
orient sky

And then the famous Flying Fortress took off bristling with guns
and testosterone to make the world safe for peace and capitalism
but the birds of peace were nowhere to be found before or after
Hiroshima

And so then clever men built bigger and faster flying machines and
these great man-made birds with jet plumage flew higher than any
real birds and seemed about to fly into the sun and melt their wings
and like Icarus crash to earth

And the Wright brothers were long forgotten in the high-flying
bombers that now began to visit their blessings on various Third
Worlds all the while claiming they were searching for doves of
peace

And they kept flying and flying until they flew right into the 21st
century and then one fine day a Third World struck back and
stormed the great planes and flew them straight into the beating
heart of Skyscraper America where there were no aviaries and no
parliaments of doves and in a blinding flash America became a part
of the scorched earth of the world

And a wind of ashes blows across the land
And for one long moment in eternity
There is chaos and despair
And buried loves and voices
Cries and whispers
Fill the air
Everywhere

PITY THE NATION
(After Khalil Gibran)

Pity the nation whose people are sheep
and whose shepherds mislead them
Pity the nation whose leaders are liars
Whose sages are silenced
and whose bigots haunt the airwaves
Pity the nation that raises not its voice
but aims to rule the world
by force and by torture
And knows
no other language but its own
Pity the nation whose breath is money
and sleeps the sleep of the too well fed
Pity the nation Oh pity the people of my country
My *country, tears of thee*
Sweet land of liberty!

SOUTH OF THE BORDER

Gringos and gringas in beach chairs
        slurping down the margaritas
     and listening to the mariachis
          and their thumping guitarrones
And never ever hearing
    the distant drums of the dispossessed
       where promises made in the plazas
          are betrayed in the back country

DRAGON'S TEETH

A headless man is running
down the street
He is carrying his head
in his hands
A woman runs after him
She has his heart
in her hands
And the drones keep coming
And those people keep running
down the dirt streets
Not the same two people
but thousands of others & brothers
All running from the drones
sowing pure hate
and for every drone that zeroes in
on these running people
up spring a thousand Bin Ladens
a thousand new terrorists
Like dragon's teeth sown
From which armed warriors spring up
Crying for blood & revenge

WITH BECKETT

I dreamt I saw Samuel Beckett last night
walking through the little park
behind the dark brooding hulk
of the cathedral of Notre Dame
where the leaves of the *marronniers*
quivered in the rain
He was wearing a worn tweed coat
with collar turned up
And I imagined he had just come
from the Théâtre de la Poche
where they had just played in French
the thousandth performance of "Waiting for Godot"
And he sat down on a wet bench
and pretended to cry as he laughed
and pretended to laugh as he cried

And I was with him sitting there
under the chestnut trees
mon semblable mon frère!

AT SEA

(for Pablo Neruda)

The sea through the trees
      distant
        shining
The dark foreground
          a stone wall
            with lichen
An old salt
      sits staring out
         at the sea
A wind sways the palms
         infrequently
Another day prepares
        for heat and silence
A small plane
      buzzing like a fly
        disturbs the sky
The air eats it

Far out on the slumbering sea
          a trawler creeps along
The wind from the south
      blows the bait in the fish's mouth

The yawning sea
         swallows the trawler
The lichen lives on
      in its volcanic stone
            taciturn
              eternal
    awaiting its turn
         in the turn of the sun
Never will I return here
    never again
       breathe this wind
         on this far run
       in the reaches of morning
    where the sea whispers
         patience and salt
The sun
   scorches the sky
       and drops like a burnt-out match
         into night
And I am an animal still
     perhaps once a bird
     a halcyon
    who makes its nest at sea
  on my little flight across
      the little chart
        of my existence
Life goes on
      full of silence and clamor
    in the grey cities

in the far bourgs
in the white cities by the sea
where I go on
writing my life
in neither blood nor wine
I still await an epiphany
by the petri-dish of the sea
where all life began
by swimming
But it's time now
to give an accounting of everything
an explanation of everything
such as
why there is darkness at night
Everywhere the sea is rising
Am I to be drowned
with the rest of them
all the animals of earth
washed away in ocean
motherer and moitherer
in this tremendous moment
of calamitous sea-change
as our little world disappears
in a tremor of ocean and fear
to the murmur
of the middle mind of America
as imbeciles in neckties
drop from the trees?
No matter then

if I end up
in a house of insurgents
on the Avenida de los Insurgentes
or shoeless on Boston Common
or cast-up clueless
in my great Uncle Désir's
beach hut
in St. Thomas
Pardon my conduct then
if I can't give you
any final word—
a final unified theory of existence—
all thought subsumed
in one great thought
(utopian vision!)
Humans with all their voices
as myriad as
the syllables of the sea
have never been able to fathom
man's fate
nor tell us why we are here
Still will we be
free as the sea
to be nothing but
our own shadow selves
beach bums all after all
in future time when
nations no longer exist

and the earth is swept
by ethnic hordes
in search of food and shelter?
Neither patient nor placid
in the face of all this
in the sea of every day
with its two tides
I run before the wind
immune to hidden reefs or harbors
Someone throws me
crystal fruits
in the shape of life-preservers
Others wave
from distant strands
Goodbye! Goodbye!
Beached at last
bleached out
I would to the woods again
with its ancient trees
that sing like sitars
in the wind
Wordless ragas!
Shipwrecked ashore
at the mercy of avaricious gulls—
And yet and yet
we are still not born for despair
Spring comes anyway
And a gay excursion train appears

The ancient conductor
            with stove-pipe hat
                and gold pocketwatch
            greets us like long-lost passengers
                gracing us with
                        wreathes around our necks
            as arms of lovers
                insanely embrace us
Is there anything more to be said
        before they carry us off
                        as dead
        while we're still dreaming
    still in search
            of the bread of the word
                        cast upon the waters
        the dough that rises
            in the yeast of speech
                in the written word
                        in poetry
Tracks upon the sand!
        left by corralled bands of animals
            cornered by mistakes and habitudes
                and trains taken
                    to mistaken destinations
                        or trips taken or not taken
                            with angels of love
                                to lower latitudes

Between two waves
       the ocean is still—
           a silence of ages
      lasting but a moment
         between two waves
          of emotion
    as lovers
        turn to each other
              or away
    Love ebbs and flows
         comes and goes
        between two emotions
      but surges forth again
      with each new wave
  as some sea-creature from the deep
        breaks the surface with a leap!
The sea roars but says no more
O the yarns it could spin
    if it would
        between its rages
  under the eye of the sun
      under the ear of the sky—
        Plunderers and pieces of eight!
    Invisible cities!
        Crystal skulls!
              Petrified hulls!
     Sailors' masturbations!

or yesterday's sperm
                lost in the wake
                        of a pleasure boat
O endless the inchoate
        incoherent narrative— Voyageur, pass on!
We are not our fathers
                yet we carry on
                        breathing like them
                                loving and killing like them
Away then away
                in our great tall ships
        over the hills of ocean
    to where Atlantis
                still rides the tides
    or where that magic mountain
                        not on any map
                        wreathed in radiance
                                still hides

                                    BELIZE, 2/2010